613
IVE

Iveson-Iveson, Joan.

Your health.

33197000039128

$9.90

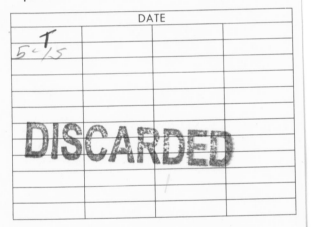

DATE			
T 5/15			
DISCARDED			

YOUR HEALTH

Joan Iveson-Iveson

Illustrated by Bill Donohoe

The Bookwright Press
New York · 1986

All About You

Your Eyes
Your Hands and Feet
Your Health
Your Nose and Ears
Your Skin and Hair
Your Teeth

Acknowledgments

Sally and Richard Greenhill p.5, 6, 9, 12, 15, 16, 17, 19, 23; J. Merrett p.14; Wayland Picture Library p.20.

First published in the United States in 1986 by
The Bookwright Press
387 Park Avenue South
New York, NY 10016

First published in 1985 by Wayland (Publishers) Limited
61 Western Road, Hove, East Sussex BN3 1JD, England
© 1985 Wayland (Publishers) Limited

Second impression 1986

ISBN 0–531–18044–1
Library of Congress Catalog Card Number: 85–72747

Phototypeset by Kalligraphics Limited, Redhill, Surrey
Printed in Italy by G. Canale and C.S.p.A., Turin

Contents

What is health?

It is difficult to say exactly what your health is. If you are healthy you feel happy and contented and your body is strong and fights off illnesses.

Unlike our **ancestors** we now expect to lead long, healthy lives, free from disease. Modern medical care can help us recover from all kinds of illnesses and repair broken bones, but there is also a lot we can do every day to keep ourselves healthy.

Your health is not only affected by the **environment** in which you live but also by the way in which you live. Taking care of your body by keeping it clean, eating a well-balanced diet, having regular check-ups at the dentist, getting regular exercise, never smoking cigarettes, relaxing and sleeping well, will all lead to a life of good health.

What is hygiene?

If you follow the rules of hygiene you will lead a clean and healthy life. One of the first rules of hygiene is to wash yourself every day. This is because you need to wash away the dead **cells**, and the sweat and oil from your skin. If you don't wash every day you will soon begin to smell unpleasant.

It is important that you change and wash your clothes regularly. Your clothes absorb many of the **secretions** from your body, and so they need to be cleaned, particularly socks and underwear. Wearing fresh, clean clothes is all part of feeling happy and well.

When you touch anything with your hands you will touch lots of tiny little germs called **bacteria** as well. Some bacteria can make you ill, and so it is important to wash your hands, especially before you eat.

7

Your hair and your teeth

Your hair should be washed quite often. At the base of every hair on your head there is a tiny **gland** which releases oil onto your skin. The oil is a natural **lubricant** but if it is allowed to stay on the hair for a long time it will begin to smell.

Brush or comb your hair regularly to remove dust and dead hairs. If you find you have **dandruff** use a mild shampoo. If it is

very bad you should ask your doctor for
advice. If you catch **head lice** your doctor
will give you a lotion that will get rid of them.

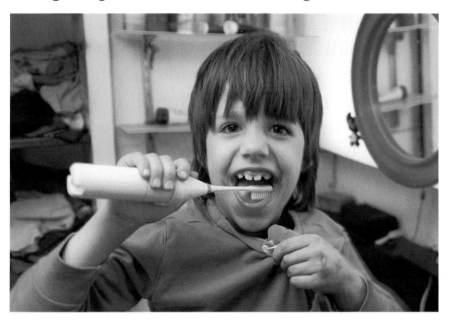

Do you always clean your teeth properly?
Brushing your teeth twice a day is very
important to fight tooth decay. You should
brush the outsides, insides and the chewing
surfaces. Plaque is the sticky stuff that makes
holes in your teeth, and this is what you are
brushing away.

Your diet

Food gives you **energy**. To keep yourself
healthy and full of energy you need to eat a
balanced diet. This means eating foods that
contain the right amounts of **carbohydrates**
for energy, **proteins** for bodybuilding,
minerals and **vitamins** to keep your body
strong and well.

In this picture you can see which foods are important to your diet. Fresh or frozen vegetables are much better for you than canned ones. **Wholewheat bread** is better for you than white bread. Always eat plenty of fresh fruit and when you feel like a snack try eating something like a bag of nuts and raisins instead of candy.

Some people are vegetarians. This means that they don't eat meat, for religious reasons perhaps, or because they don't like the idea of killing animals for food. You can have a very healthy diet without eating meat.

Sugar and fat

You do not need to eat many dairy foods or much sugar and salt. Lots of sugar is used in many of your foods such as cakes, cookies, candy, fizzy drinks and even tomato ketchup. Try not to eat candy or cookies between meals. Too much sugar will make you fat as well as harm your teeth.

The foods in this picture contain a lot of fat and sugar. Dairy foods are fatty foods. They are all those products made from cow's milk, such as butter, cheese and cream. Fast foods, such as hotdogs or hamburgers, tend to contain a lot of fat, too, because they are often fried. Snack foods, such as potato chips and peanuts, are often high in fats and salt. Try eating unsalted nuts instead.

You need a little fat every day to give you energy but too much fat will be stored in your body and will make you put on weight.

Getting exercise

Getting lots of exercise helps make your body stronger. It ensures that all the different parts of your body are supplied with the right amounts of **oxygen** and foodstuffs that are vital for it to work well.

When you are running, your muscles take more oxygen from the blood than usual. This makes you breathe faster to take in more oxygen. At the end of a running race you pant because you are having to replace the oxygen used up by your muscles.

Cramps can be the painful result of exercising at the wrong time, which may cause muscle **spasms**. It is not wise to go swimming after you have eaten. Your energy is needed to digest your food which means you may feel weaker and less able to swim.

Exercise uses up a lot of your energy. If you go on exercising without a rest, your muscles will produce a milky liquid called lactic acid. This process is painful and is what we call a stitch. When you rest, this liquid is removed by the blood, and the pain that you were feeling goes away.

16

Regular exercise prevents your joints and your **muscles** from becoming stiff. If you are unused to getting exercise you can damage your muscles if, for example, you suddenly go swimming or play tennis. So always do a little exercise every day and this will help you feel well.

Your sleep

Everybody needs to rest and to sleep. The number of hours of sleep needed varies from person to person, but on the average, two hours of rest each day and seven to eight hours of sleep each night is enough.

When you go to sleep you go through different **phases** of sleep. One phase of shallow sleep is called rapid eye movement sleep, during which time you dream. After this shallow, dreaming sleep you fall into a deep sleep.

You need to sleep so that your body can rebuild its strength for another day. It is not a good idea to eat or drink a lot just before you go to bed because this will disturb the regular pattern of your sleep. It is important also to spend some time during the day resting. Try relaxing by reading a book, like the boy in the picture.

Taking care of your health

This book has shown you how to lead a healthy life. This means more than just being well, it means being active, being happy, having a sparkle in your eyes, having shiny hair and a clear skin. There's a lot to remember so here are a few ideas to help you.

Caring for your health means:

Eating an apple or some nuts, rather than candy, when you feel like a snack.
Brushing your teeth twice a day.
Resting for a short time each day.
Washing every day.
Getting plenty of exercise.
Making sure that you have enough sleep, so that you are fully rested.
Going to the dentist every six months.

Not caring for your health means:

Eating lots of sweet things like candy or drinking sweet fizzy drinks.
Eating a bag of potato chips on the way home from school.
Brushing your teeth in ten seconds with an old, worn-out toothbrush.
Forgetting to wash your hands after you've been to the toilet or before eating a meal.
Not bothering to wash your hair when it gets dirty.
Avoiding sports.
Staying up to watch television when you should be in bed.

Glossary

Ancestors People who lived in the centuries before us; our forefathers.

Bacteria Tiny one-celled animals which cannot be seen with the naked eye. Some bacteria cause disease.

Carbohydrates Starches and sugars found in foods such as potatoes, bread and cake.

Cells Your body is made up of several millions of cells. They are very small, and they are the basic units of living matter.

Dandruff Flakes of dried skin on your scalp.

Energy The strength to do things.

Environment Your surroundings.

Gland A part of the body that lets out different liquids, such as sweat or oil.

Head lice Tiny insects, which live in human hair.

Lubricant Grease or oil.

Minerals Substances, such as iron, that your body needs in small amounts to stay healthy.

Muscle Bundles of fibers, which cause movement in your body.

Oxygen A gas that makes up part of the air we breathe.

Phase A stage in development; a period of time.

Proteins These are found in foods such as meat,

fish, eggs, milk, nuts and beans.

Secretions Liquids released from the body.

Spasm A jerk of the muscles, which you cannot control.

Vitamins A group of substances that are not made naturally in the body but are found in certain foods. They are an important part of a good diet.

Wholewheat bread Bread made from flour that has been ground from whole grain, without removing the husks.

Index